**JAZZ-AGE
BOOMTOWN**

D1539601

Jazz-Age Boomtown

JERRY L. RODNITZKY
&
SHIRLEY R. RODNITZKY

TEXAS A&M UNIVERSITY PRESS

College Station

All photographs courtesy Basil Clemons Photograph Collection,
Special Collections Division,
The University of Texas at Arlington Libraries.

The paper used in this book meets the minimum requirements
of the American National Standard for Permanence
of Paper for Printed Library Materials, Z39.48-1984.
Binding materials have been chosen for durability.

Library of Congress Cataloging-in-Publication Data

Rodnitzky, Jerome L., 1936–
    Jazz-age boomtown / Jerry Rodnitzky and Shirley Rodnitzky. — 1st ed.
        p.   cm. — (The Charles and Elizabeth Prothro Texas photography series ;
    no. 5)
    Includes bibliographical references (p.   ) and index.
    ISBN 0-89096-757-1
    1. Breckenridge (Tex.)—Social life and customs—Pictorial works. 2. Popular
culture—Texas—Breckenridge—History—20th century—Pictorial works.
3. Breckenridge (Tex.)—History—Pictorial works. 4. Petroleum industry and
trade—Texas—Breckenridge—History—20th century—Pictorial works.
5. Clemons, Basil. 6. University of Texas at Arlington—Photograph collections.
7. Photograph collections—Texas—Arlington. I. Rodnitzky, Shirley R. (Shirley
Reiger), 1941– . II. Title. III. Series.
F394.B78R63   1997
976.4´546—dc21
                                                                        96-52031
                                                                        CIP

For Joan Baez Rodnitzky,

Mark Kennedy Rodnitzky,

and Shanna Kee Anderson Rodnitzky

—Part of a New Generation of Texans

CONTENTS

PREFACE

The Basil Clemons Photograph Collection was purchased in June, 1985 by the University of Texas at Arlington with a generous grant from Vicki Vinson of Fort Worth, Texas. The Clemons photos were discovered by Jan Hart, a Breckenridge native. She told Charles Colley, then director of Special Collections Division at the university libraries, that Clemons family members had offered the collection for sale. He mentioned this to Jenkins Garrett, a key supporter and benefactor of Special Collections, who in turn brought the collection to the attention of Johnny Vinson, a Fort Worth oilman. Vinson was immediately interested in the photos, since he had grown up near Breckenridge, had later produced oil there, and had even known Clemons. Johnny Vinson, Jenkins Garrett, and Charles Colley then flew in Vinson's private plane to Commerce, Texas, to inspect the photographs. Vinson was very impressed by the collection and thought they had historical value. He invited his daughter, Vicki Vinson, who had extensive education and training in art history, to look over the collection. She was also impressed by the photographs and thought they had considerable artistic and historical value. Ms. Vinson urged the University to buy the collection without further delay, and she generously donated the funds to purchase the photographs.

The collection, dating from 1919 through 1948, includes approximately 12,000 black-and-white, silver-gelatin prints and 5,900 cellulose nitrate, acetate, and paper negatives. Most of the prints and negatives were taken in the 1920s, during which an oil boom transformed Breckenridge, Texas, from a sleepy town to a raucous, multifaceted city. Almost all the photo scenes are set in and around Breckenridge and Stephens County, but a few are set in adjacent Palo Pinto County. Perhaps ten early 1920s prints are from Clemons's work in Alaska and the Seattle, Washington, area.

After an initial display of the collection for several interested parties and university officials, staff member Betsey Hudon made a preliminary count and examination. In 1986, Shirley Rodnitzky, a special collections archivist, was assigned to arrange and house the photographs and compile a collection finding aid that broadly listed the collection's contents. The prints had been roughly organized by Clemons family members and were transferred to the library in numerous typing paper boxes, which had housed the collection since Basil Clemons's death in 1964.

Most of the photographs had been briefly described and dated by Clemons with his trademark India ink offset style. The black ink shows up white on the photographs, which helped to facilitate processing the collection. The individual prints were usually left in the subject categories arranged by the family members, since they knew more about where unidentified and/or undated items should logically be placed. Duplicate prints were separated into another series for display use and loans to other libraries or museums. The negatives vary in size, but are primarily 8" x 10" cellulose nitrate film. Since the negatives came disorganized, they had to be matched to fit the subject organization. Several hundred negatives lacked prints, and these negatives comprise a separate subseries of the negative series.

Shirley found many of Clemons's photos striking, interesting, and unique—especially those from the 1920s. She often mentioned the collection to her husband, Jerry Rodnitzky, a professor of history at The University of Texas at Arlington who specializes in twentieth-century American culture. After viewing the collection, he began planning a photo-essay book about 1920s Breckenridge as a boomtown based on Clemons's photographs. He was particularly impressed by how these photographs often illustrated the first truly national American culture shaped by mass media. Basil Clemons's photographs also often reflected the transformation of rural to urban values in the early twentieth century. And, of course, they directly documented the vivid drama of an oil boomtown.

In their first joint scholarly work, the Rodnitzkys divided the tasks: Jerry searched the Special Collections Division and elsewhere for material on Basil Clemons and Breckenridge and compiled the text; Shirley organized the photographs and identified the collection's best prints. Together they narrowed the photo choices for specific chapters and wrote photo captions.

This book is primarily a photographic essay about a West Texas oil boomtown. It is neither a biography of Basil Clemons nor a history of Breckenridge. On a larger scale, however, the book is a photographic record of the cultural roots of modern America. Whatever dates mark the beginning of recent or contemporary America, most historians would agree that modern American culture began after World War I and took shape in the 1920s. The twenties featured such modern cultural fare as widespread auto ownership, big-time sports, and the first mesmerizing mass media—radio and cinema. Basil Clemons never saw himself as the photographer of modern American culture, but that is what he has become for us. His photographs will remain American—and Texas—treasures, because they so vividly captured that formative modern, national, Jazz-Age culture.

ACKNOWLEDGMENTS

The authors wish to thank the staffs of the Breckenridge Public Library, the Swenson Museum in Breckenridge, and the Special Collections Division of The University of Texas at Arlington Libraries for their help. Thanks are also due to Gerald D. Saxon, assistant director for Special Collections, for his help and encouragement, and to the University Media Services staff for the time and care they invested in reproducing Clemons's work. A very special note of thanks must go to Ms. Vicki Vinson for the additional generous grant that aided this book's publication.

In the 1920s, Breckenridge was the stereotypical West Texas boomtown. When oil was discovered near Breckenridge in 1917, it was a sleepy town of perhaps 500, but when the oil boom accelerated in January 1920, the population reached 1500. Within little more than two years, however, Breckenridge's population swelled to nearly thirty thousand, as its evermore plentiful crude oil eventually fetched $3.00 a barrel.

Suddenly, ranchers around Breckenridge became oilmen. Public school teachers left their jobs to become oil wildcatters, and enterprising businessmen moved in to provide the thriving population with sustenance, housing, and entertainment. Oil derricks dotted the landscape, appearing in many backyards and even in the commercial districts. Breckenridge boomed between World Wars I and II. It also boomed between two federal censuses: the 1920 census was too early to catch the boom years, and the 1930 census was too late.

By 1930, the oil-price crash and the national economic collapse had largely deflated Breckenridge's economy. Moreover, after the first early, chaotic years, Breckenridge's affluent, permanent citizens took control and tamed its wilder, boomtown ways. In 1922, for example, just two years after the rampant growth started, Breckenridge citizens built both a modern junior high and an even more substantial modern high school. Slowly Breckenridge changed from a roughneck oil boomtown to a vigorous commercial city of schools, churches, and modern housing. Breckenridge's professionals and businessmen wanted a city safe for their families. In the early 1920s, some had left their families in Fort Worth or elsewhere, but by the mid-1920s, Breckenridge was a microcosm of Fort Worth, Abilene, and other Texas urban centers.

In the 1990s, one can experience all the excitement that was boomtown Breckenridge through Basil Clemons's photographs. Clemons came to Breckenridge with the oil boom in 1919. He had been a photographer in Hollywood, Seattle, and Alaska and also served in World War I. Clemons would spend the rest of his life photographing Breckenridge through times both good and bad. His 1920s photographs are especially interesting because Breckenridge changed so much during that decade. Clemons's photos of cultural life are particularly valuable, because boomtowns such as Breckenridge were where national urban culture and small-town America met and melded in the 1920s. The new local cinemas, that we call the first picture shows, and the live traveling shows were the first cultural bridges to transform rural and urban America into a homogenous, mass culture. Clemons's camera was there at the moment of creation to leave us a still-frame picture show of the vibrant Jazz Age.

JAZZ-AGE BOOMTOWN

CHAPTER 1

Basil Clemons:
The Photographer and the Man

Many people knew Basil Edwin Clemons the town photographer, but few knew the man. We may never know the real Basil Clemons, but only that part revealed in his work and lifestyle. His vocation seemed to be his life, since those who knew Clemons consistently claim that photography was his only vital interest. Such single-mindedness should have made Clemons a commercially successful small-town photographer. Yet, throughout his thirty-odd years in Breckenridge, Texas, Clemons lived in a six-by-ten-foot tent wagon in near poverty.[1] He lived simply and close to nature.

Clemons was in many ways a Texas-style Thoreau, but he adapted his philosophy late in life. He started as a wanderer. The eldest of seventeen children, Clemons was born July 22, 1887, in Lauderdale County, Alabama. He attended elementary school in Alabama until 1900, when the family moved to Ridgeway in East Texas. In 1903, at age sixteen, Clemons left home for California, where he experienced the San Francisco earthquake in 1906. He then moved to Hollywood, where he learned his photographic trade. There he first worked as a cinema photographer and later joined the traveling Tom Mix Wild West Show. In 1910, Clemons moved to Alaska, where his work included the first aerial photographs of that territory and photographs of the gold rush. He served as a private in the Army during World War I and was briefly stationed at Fort Liscom, Alaska. After the war he moved to Seattle, Washington, where he started his own photography studio. Indeed, his earliest Breckenridge photographs show his Seattle studio logo. By 1919, the restless Clemons was touring with a traveling circus, and while home in Texas, he was notified that his Seattle studio had been destroyed by a fire. He then followed the oil boom to Breckenridge, Texas, late in 1919 and became the town photographer. Clemons spent the rest of his life in Breckenridge, dying there in 1964, about fifteen years after retiring from the photography business.[2]

Though Breckenridge was booming in the 1920s, Clemons's business showed little prosperity. His home and studio remained a wagon, formerly used as a ranch cookshack, situated on a vacant lot in town. Financial gain or national fame did not seem to interest Clemons. In 1936, he supposedly received a written offer from Eastman Kodak for the secret of a color process he had developed earlier, but Clemons never pursued the Kodak offer. He seemed in rebellion against technology, even though he worked on the frontier of photographic science and used a stripped Model-T Ford to travel to his photo shoots. For example, he mixed darkroom chemicals by taste rather than exact measurement, which suggests that Clemons saw photography as an art rather than a science.[3]

Like many artistic Bohemians, Clemons was a study in contrasts. He drove a car but lived in a primitive wagon. He ate simple natural foods, often cooked over a fire, yet he worked with sophisticated chemical formulas and processes in his photography. Perhaps the biggest irony was his work for the many town boosters that made Breckenridge a boomtown in the twenties. The "go-getters," parodied by Sinclair Lewis in his novel *Main Street,* were also on Breckenridge's main streets. And there was Clemons, the social misfit, in the midst of them—taking photos that promoted small businesses and taking family photos of newly prosperous citizens.

Yet, Clemons was hardly a pawn of Breckenridge's affluent businessmen. He covered every event, regardless of the social strata or ethnic group involved. Clemons shot class photos for the public schools and provided work portraits of oil derrick laborers. He shot wedding pictures on weekends and covered town fires at night. He supplied the town's newspaper with news and booster photos. Clemons also covered the increasing stream of cultural and entertainment events that passed through Breckenridge, from rodeos to circuses.

His photos are generally not works of art: His portraits lack the intensity of an Edward Steichen, and his news shots lack the poignant timing of a Margaret Bourke-White. His landscapes lack the artistic angles and juxtapositions of an Ansel Adams. What Clemons's photos do offer, however, is stark social reality. They tell us simply what the past was like and not what it meant to Clemons. This has its own charm and value—especially for the historian (or anyone) trying to make sense of human experience.

Of all his photos, those that depicted circus performers are the liveliest. Clemons seemed to have a special rapport with circus people, perhaps because of his association with them prior to settling down in Breckenridge. There is a special charm in the way they posed for his camera. Perhaps they sensed that Clemons, like them, was off-beat and on the edge of civilization. Having traveled with both a circus and wild west show when younger, the circus may have represented youth, freedom, and the open road to an aging photographer, tied to a small town.

When he photographed western shows and rodeos, Clemons's stark, straightforward posing worked against the cowboy myth. His photos capture the uneasiness with which contemporary sheriffs and cowboys viewed the increasingly urban and modern Texas landscapes. Clemons's cowboys seem frozen out of time, not captured in their own time.

Clemons's friendships formed a composite of his life and work. He had friends in every economic, social, ethnic, and age group: bankers and businessmen, workers and young students. Rich and poor, male and female, Anglo, African-American, Mexican-American, young and old, beautiful and plain, native or traveler—all seemed to find Clemons fascinating or just good company.[4]

His self-portraits suggest his personality. The Clemons of the 1920s—with his trendy jodhpur pants and high-laced boots—looks confident, comfortably Bohemian, and at peace with himself. Since he had little apparent ambition, he obviously did not threaten people. Here was an interesting, original character, with whom one did not have to compete. Clemons knew almost everyone in town and was universally liked, although his scruffy clothes and intense expressions sometimes scared children. The Clemons-as-Bohemian legend probably fed itself by word of mouth.

When oil prices fell in the late 1920s and Breckenridge crashed with the rest of America in the Depression, Clemons was, ironically, suddenly at the center of social experience. Clemons had been in an economic depression of his own since he had come to Breckenridge, but the nation had just caught up with his lifestyle against its will. As his lifestyle became less unique, Clemons became less exotic and more common. What happened to Clemons also affected many urban Jazz-Age Bohemians. Their high-profile and willing rejection of material wealth in the 1920s became an involuntary, economic nightmare for many Americans in the 1930s.

Through it all, Clemons pushed on. The small town photographer became a smaller town photographer as Breckenridge's population decreased from a 1920s height of thirty thousand to around six thousand in the 1930s. Clemons's camera still caught it all—the sick small businesses, the depressed faces, and the suddenly relaxed townscape. A couple of movie theaters remained, but Breckenridge was now off the beaten track for circuses and rodeos, and soon it became a cultural appendage of Fort Worth and Abilene. Yet life had not changed for Clemons. He still slept in the open air, near his wagon studio, and roamed the town and countryside, shooting everything that moved and many things that did not. His lenses covered Breckenridge until 1949, when failing eyesight forced him to retire. Eventually, he went totally blind. He died in poverty in 1964, yet his photographs contain a rich legacy.

Clemons was indeed somewhat of a latter-day Texas Thoreau. After two decades of youthful roaming, Clemons found peace in an interesting Texas town. When Henry David Thoreau wrote that "a man is rich in proportion to the number of things which he can afford to leave alone," he seems to describe Clemons's philosophy of living. Thoreau drove life into a corner at Walden Pond and noted that he had "traveled a good deal in Concord." Similarly, Clemons had traveled a good deal in Breckenridge and Stephens County. His early years in Breckenridge were the wildest—if not the widest—of his travels, and Clemons's 1920s photos are by far his most exciting work.

Basil Clemons in bed in his tent-wagon. When weather permitted,
he often slept outside under a tree, ca. 1925.

Basil Clemons using his crystal radio set—the first such set in Breckenridge, 1920.

Self-portrait of Basil Clemons and a friend harvesting corn that
had been planted on Labor Day for a Thanksgiving feast.
Clemons is wearing his trademark jodhpur pants, 1934.

Basil Clemons standing among his belongings on the vacant lot
that he called home, 1941.

CHAPTER 2

West Texas Crude:
Breckenridge as an Oil Boomtown

Texas' first commercial-scale oil strike took place in 1894 in Corsicana, in Navarro County, fifty miles south of Dallas. It happened while the city was drilling for water. Yet Texas never became a major oil producer until the massive Spindletop strike of 1901, near Beaumont in the Southeast Texas coastal region. Further discoveries around the Texas Gulf area excited prospectors, and by 1910, wildcatters roamed the state. The West Texas oil era started in 1917 with the discovery of oil in Ranger, in Eastland County. This strike came precisely as World War I increased America's oil hunger. By 1920, West Texas oil had also been discovered in Burkburnett, Breckenridge, and Desdemona, in that order. By 1928, other discoveries had made Texas the leading oil-producing state.[1]

The first Breckenridge gusher came in 1918. By 1920, the Breckenridge fields produced fifty million barrels annually—more than that produced by all of Louisiana. Soon wooden derricks dotted the countryside and even invaded the city, where derricks in streets and backyards were soon followed by tents on vacant lots to house oilfield workers and their families. Breckenridge became largely a tent city, strangely appropriate in the newly created circus atmosphere of a boomtown.

Fortune hunters descended on Breckenridge in 1918 to search for black gold, just as real gold had drawn adventurers to California seventy years earlier. Oil and mining boomtowns had similar problems, mostly the result of overpopulation. They shared the inevitable benefits and drawbacks that follow instant wealth. In Breckenridge businesses of all kinds boomed, but so did crime and vice, especially bootlegging. Construction boomed as well, but the hastily constructed houses and flimsy tents caused periodic, devastating fires that were especially dangerous amidst producing city oil wells. Indeed, most city fires were caused by gas and oil, which leaked undetected from unregulated wells.[2]

Yet, economic progress was easily measured. In 1920, Stephens County had thirteen banks, and Breckenridge alone had two banks, seventeen gas stations, seventy-three grocery stores, twenty-seven rooming houses and hotels, forty-three restaurants, eight lumberyards, two newspapers, twenty-two barbers, fifteen physicians, and fifty-two lawyers. In one year the population went from 1,500 to 20,000 and, eventually, to almost 30,000 in the mid-twenties. R.C. Richman, an area resident, describes a typical Breckenridge Sunday in 1920 with typical small-town prose:

> Nothing but merchandise stores closed for the day and the brothels of the city did a land office business. From late Saturday night . . . the streets of the town would be packed with a weaving, sweating mob of men, tanned and virile, loose as to morals and careless of companions, looking for surcease from the deadly routine of the week. And it was to be found . . . all of the gamblers, disorderly housekeepers, ex-saloon men—all of that train of camp followers of the great God 'Oil' were to be found entrenched on every street . . . offering their services to the pleasure seeking mob. They did a flourishing business as did the hooch-houses, 'jake joints' and even the one or two 'hop joints'. . . . Especially did gambling flourish, for the oil fraternity as a whole is a gambling set.[3]

Richman also describes Breckenridge as seen from a distance. "It was an eerie scene. The town was in full glare from lights of every description. There were flaming gasoline torches, blinking yellow gas jets, electric lights strung here and there with abandon. . . . The noise was terrific for a sleeping city—or one that should have been at this time of night. The car roared past the first few tents and we were on Breckenridge's main thoroughfare."[4]

Eventually the new oil barons and the original community leaders combined to bring order out of chaos. Breckenridge remained somewhat of a roughneck city, but also an increasingly well-managed enterprise. Fire hazards were lessened, criminals were apprehended and educational and cultural opportunities were even enhanced. Max Goldblatt, a Breckenridge teenager in the 1920s, felt that the city was kept civilized and cultured by a core of older residents. These ranchers and store owners accepted change and benefitted from the new wealth, but they insisted that money be invested in public institutions and amenities.[5]

From schools to hospitals and local fairs to community theater, these town boosters kept Breckenridge from becoming just another boomtown. Partly out of pride, partly for self-preservation, they nourished the town's continuing culture and humanity. The boomtown specter haunted Breckenridge's respectable leaders. They protected their own personal image as much as the town's.

Through it all, Clemons's camera caught everything in oil-drenched black and white. At first, the muddy new streets and hastily erected new buildings made Breckenridge look like a Hollywood western movie set. The in-town derricks made it appear that Breckenridge had been built amidst an oil field, instead of the reverse. Indeed, from airplanes, boomtown Breckenridge looked more like an oil field than a town.

The city of Breckenridge "and its founts of liquid gold," 1922.

Panoramic view of Breckenridge, Texas, northwest
of the Courthouse Dome, 1925.

Dyer Street and its complement of tent housing, 1920.

Breckenridge street crews trying to provide harder surfaces
for daring auto drivers on East Walker Street, ca. 1921.

Walker Street, the main commercial avenue, before a devastating fire
the same night this photo was taken, 1921.

Firefighters putting out another, smaller blaze at the edge of town using
the new high-pressure water system, 1921.

The Breckenridge fire chief checking the "ruins of another
notorious Breckenridge . . . fire," 1921.

The horse in the cart: "Breckenridge, Texas, where horses ride in Fords," 1927.

Breckenridge High School and students amidst a sea of oil wells.
Students are waging a campaign for Polish relief in Europe, 1922.

A rancher and his horse, reflected in the foreground, while encroaching modern technology (auto and derricks) loom in the background. This photo shows Clemons's considerable, but seldom-demonstrated artistic ability, 1926.

Investors in "The Triangle Block Oil Syndicate" meet at oil well, 1920.

The costs of technology and progress: a polluted, garbage-littered
stream near oil derricks, 1922.

A new Breckenridge home, complete with its own oil well, 1923.

CHAPTER 3

Bread and Circuses:
Entertainment off and on the Road

Breckenridge's boom brought not only oil entrepreneurs and oil companies, but cultural promoters as well. For the first time, circuses and wild west shows put Breckenridge on their itinerary. Also, traveling dramatic shows, dance troupes, and bands began adding the city to their regular circuit. Breckenridge suddenly became a cultural oasis in what once had been an arid, cultural wasteland. The circuses, wild west shows, and musical acts gave people the classic 1920s cultural seat. Citizens no longer had to travel to seek the strange and exotic; increasingly everything came to them.

When we look at these photographs, the circuses that visited then seem to us timeless and contemporary. Indeed, the unchanging traditions that circuses continually brought to smaller towns and bigger cities are what kept them viable then and keep them entertaining now. Each generation brought its children to see and enjoy what they had experienced as children. Adult circus patrons came to see the familiar and not the exotic.

Circus historians present the circus as a unique entertainment, separate from related amusements. In the twentieth century, circus people did tend to look down on carnival and other traveling entertainers as inferior. Circus people not only traveled together, they lived together, representing a community on the move as surely as wagon trains to the West once did. Circus people lived in isolation from society and faced general hostility from outsiders. Whether freak performers or skill performers, circus entertainers were often considered oddities. The circus world returned this hostility semantically by referring to customers as "rube," "mark," "yokel," or even "sucker."[1]

Basil Clemons had an obvious and special feel for circus people. Almost certainly his rapport stemmed directly from the years that he traveled with circuses as a young man. His circus subjects exude a warmth and naturalness seldom seen in photographs taken by more famous photographers. Certainly, the circus portraits are special treasures among Clemons's photographs.

Besides the classic circus, Breckenridge also saw the unique one-man shows. The lone barnstorming pilot, the world's strongest man, the nation's fastest race car driver—all competed for Breckenridge's amusement dollars. They were joined by various dance groups, theater troupes, and five-man jazz bands. These road shows enriched themselves, while claiming to bring cultural enrichment to communities. They were often the only live national culture that smaller regional towns saw.

The wild west shows were particularly (and ironically) popular. Just a few decades before, Breckenridge had been the wild West, but by the 1920s, that was all in the past. There were still ranchers around Breckenridge amid the oil fields, but the modern cowhand was no longer simply a rugged horseman. He usually spent his time driving a tractor, tending crops, harvesting hay, doing various routine jobs, and envying the costumed men working in the wild west show, who got paid a lot more than he did. Yet, the wild west show satisfied most Breckenridge citizens, by guaranteeing that they would see what they expected. The shows reinforced the patrons' own image of the old West, based more on romance than history.[2] As historian Earl Pomeroy suggests, the West as myth supplanted the historical West because the West had become Eastern and "the Westerner had become an Easterner and not merely host to Easterners." The modern Westerner wore sideburns and a ten-gallon hat to the rodeo or wild west show without quite knowing whether he did it out of civic spirit, because others expected it, or because he thought it was his cultural duty.[3] The West was a mental state that would long outlast material circumstances.

Marshall McLuhan, the cultural sociologist, has a different theory that might explain Breckenridge's preoccupation with the old West. McLuhan felt that people were generally frightened by change and, thus, they clung to the recent past. They lived in the present, while looking in the "rearview mirror."[4] They "marched backwards toward the future." Basil Clemons's camera is a rearview mirror with a memory, capturing all the entertainment and excitement that came to Breckenridge in the 1920s.

Traveling minstrel show, 1927.

Emerson Western Wild West Show, 1920.

The whole troupe of Texas Kid's traveling Frontier Days show, 1925.

Cracker Jack promotion at John Robinson Circus, 1920.

Acrobat with Robbins Brothers Circus, 1926.

The Circus Fat Lady, 1922.

Within the image, handwritten caption:

C. H. Baudendistel "Major High Pockets" Elephant Educator And Originator Of The Above Trick, Showing How Easily An Elephant Can Take A Mans Head In It's Mouth And Lift Him Up.

C. H. Baudendistel, an elephant trainer, being lifted off the ground by one of his pupils, 1926.

Circus animal trainer and Bear Cub, 1920.

Madam Rainey's Jazz Hounds, 1922. "Ma" Rainey's traveling show
gained fame later. Ma Rainey (real name Gertrude Melissa Rainey) became known
as the Mother of the Blues. Her most famous protégé, Bessie Smith,
has been called the Empress of the Blues.

Troy Snapp and Girls, Madam Rainey's Broadway Strutters, 1922.

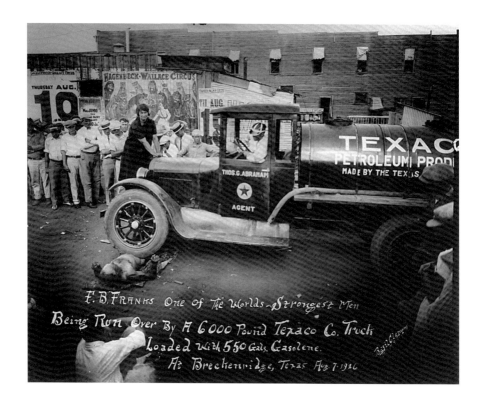

Traveling strongman, E. B. Franks, being run over by a loaded
three-ton Texaco gasoline truck, 1926.

Traveling motorcyclists in town for "Oil Derby Races," which
featured both auto and cycle racing, 1927.

Breckenridge Rodeo contestants, 1921.

Willie McGee, an African-American cowboy performer
with the United Wild West Show, 1921.

CHAPTER 4

The First Picture Show: The Impact of Cinema

In his novel, *The Last Picture Show,* Larry McMurtry used the movie theater as both a messenger from the larger outside world and a symbol of small-town decline. The action takes place during the 1950s in a West Texas oil town named Thalia. The town has been slowly declining, and when the theater closes, Thalia loses a crucial link to the national culture and suffers a heavy blow to its pride.[1]

In the 1920s Breckenridge was the reverse of Thalia. As the oil boom mushroomed and brought prosperity in its wake, it opened the door for live entertainment from the state and national road shows. More importantly, the new affluence forged a permanent bond between Breckenridge and Hollywood with the eventual establishment of three movie theaters in the early 1920s: the National, Alhambra, and Palace. These picture shows were the major cultural bridges of the mass media revolution that transformed rural and urban America into an homogeneous mass culture.

Breckenridge was a classic case study of an area culturally transformed by cinema. Suddenly national matinee idols were the new models for dress, speech, and mannerisms. National cinema corporations provided the posters that small town theaters turned into the lobby displays to lure local moviegoers. Various local promotions, from contests to raffles, helped pump attendance. Whether B-film double features or first-run national blockbusters were showing, Breckenridge citizens got the movie habit in the 1920s as surely as their big-city counterparts in Dallas, Chicago, and New York. Films created a seamless national culture. You could drive from New York to West Texas and end up in front of the same Rudolph Valentino film. The social experience of attending a movie theater and the reaction to the movie stars and films were universal, notwithstanding the size of the theater or the audience's regional makeup.[2]

Theaters did have to work against mounting Hollywood notoriety in the 1920s. The sensational news coverage of divorces of stars such as Mary Pickford and sex scandals such as the Fatty Arbuckle manslaughter case highlighted Hollywood infidelity and immorality. The notoriety rubbed off on theaters. Even the Hayes Commission, formed in 1922 to reform filmdom, did little to alter Hollywood's negative image in the twenties. Especially in smaller rural communities, church groups and parents looked on theaters with growing suspicion.[3]

Theaters sought to enhance their image by using ornate and artistic architecture. In the large cities, the movie palaces might be modeled after Greek or Egyptian temples, or at the very least, they would be filled with classic sculpture and paintings. Smaller towns, such as Breckenridge, pursued the same goal with more symbolism and less material grandeur. Small-town theaters were usually modern and classy looking, with generous use of velvety drapes and ornate tile. These theaters substituted exotic names, such as "Alhambra" and "Palace" for actual exotic architecture. The almost universal spelling of "theatre" symbolized the movie house's national quest for class and legitimacy.[4]

Theaters could also enhance towns by their number as well as their ornateness. Breckenridge's three cinemas made it a veritable West Texas cultural center. Customers often drove two hours to see an enticing film, and around the theaters there invariably grew a network of shops and eateries, which fed on the traffic drawn by Hollywood movies.

In the 1990s, Breckenridge, although theaterless, still shares in the national film culture via video stores and cable television. But the social experience associated with moviegoing, so pivotal in the 1920s, has disappeared. A film is now something you bring home in a box. However, perhaps Breckenridge has not missed that much by not having a modern movie theater. Many older, nostalgic filmgoers would not trade the once palatial theaters of Fort Worth or Dallas, or the cozy colorful movie houses of Breckenridge, for contemporary glass, multiscreen cinematic showrooms, despite their vastly enhanced film technology.

The lobby display at the National Theatre for the 1921 hit, *Passion.* The film
starred Pola Negri, a Polish-born actress whose real name was Appolonia Chalupek.
As a femme fatale she starred in many American silent films,
before talkies ended her career. Both film producers and theater chains
encouraged displays by holding national lobby display contests.

Lobby picture from the National Theatre's display for *Neptune's Bride* in 1921.
This sexploitation film invited filmgoers to ogle bathing beauties.
Like many similar silents, plot was secondary to scenery.

National Theatre display of *Blood and Sand,* starring Rudolph Valentino.
This 1922 bullfighter film came a year after Valentino became famous for his roles in
The Four Horsemen of the Apocalypse and *The Sheik.*

A best smile contest provides a human street advertisement for *Smilin Thru,* starring Norma Talmadge. This 1922 film came midway in Talmadge's career. She broke into film in 1914 at age 17 and always played a heroine; but like many silent stars could not make the transition to talkies.

Above: Lobby display for Cecil DeMille's *Adam's Rib,* 1923. DeMille, later famous
for biblical spetaculars such as *The Ten Commandments,* was known
for sexy society dramas in the 1920s. These high society films taught
rural Americans what was chic in New York City.

Opposite page: Local aspiring screen star, Ouida Wildman, won the *Fort Worth
Star-Telegram's* contest for best ready-made movie face in 1921.
Hollywood look-alikes were as common in small towns as large cities.

TEXAS GIRL HAS REAL SCREEN FACE, SAYS MISS LA[DD]

Ouida Wildman One in Thousands, Expert's Verdict

BY CONSTANCE LADD

HAVE A LOOK AT A READY-MADE MOVIE FACE

MISS WILDMAN TELLS HOW IT FEELS TO KNOW ONE HAS A MOVIE FACE

BY OUIDA WILDMAN

Ouida Wildman, 507 North Ross Avenue, Mexia, Texas, Miss Ladd discovered the first ready-made screen personality from among thousands of Star-Telegram readers who have sent in photographs. The smaller pictures around the margin show various poses of Miss Wildman. Miss Wildman's photographs, with the indorsement of Miss Ladd, will be viewed by some of the famous directors of Los Angeles, and her chances of becoming a real ready-made screen are good.

The Broken Doll

'Ridin Bob And The Totin Nash.'

Ridin' Bob Roberts, a B-Western movie star makes a 1926 appearance at
Breckenridge's Alhambra Theatre to plug his own movie. It was not
inappropriate for Roberts to endorse and ride an auto rather
than a horse. Breckenridge produced far more oil than oats.

The Indian part of the cowboy-and-Indian film motif is represented by an even dozen
young Breckenridge "braves" advertising a popular 1926 Zane Grey Western film.
Grey's stories were made into almost a hundred silent and sound films.

This 1926 street scene, with a Lon Chaney film, *Tell It to the Marines,* playing, was as close as Breckenridge got to a drive-in movie in the twenties. The two-hour parking limit gave mobile film patrons just enough time to "flick out."

In 1926, the Alhambra Theatre presents the classic movie bargain—the double feature. Double bills usually consisted of B films or older films.

An innovative 1926 street display for the film, *Why Girls Leave Home.*
Anna Nillson was a Swedish-born actress who had played American film roles
since 1911. The 65,000 girls that the display claims left home every year were likely far
less than the number of girls who saw this film weekly. Note the
three-day showing—a common sequence that fed the American film appetite
with an average two features per week.

In 1926, the National Theatre goes to great lengths to lure customers.
Their slogan might have been: "Movies Are Bigger Than Ever."

The man holding the turkey is not making a subtle comment on the
artistic merit of the National Theatre's 1926 feature film, *Take It from Me*. Rather,
he is holding the raffle prize that some lucky matinee customer
will take home. The movie giveaways, contests, and promotions
so common in the depressed 1930s were already well established in the 1920s.

The newest Breckenridge theater, The Palace, showing an ever-popular
Clara Bow film in 1929. Bow symbolized the new sexuality.
Her trademarks were "bee stung lips" and S.A. (sex appeal).

The interior of the Palace Theatre in 1929. It was not very palatial compared
to the plush theaters in the big cities, but not shabby either. Note that the
Theatre had a real stage that could be used for live performances.

CHAPTER 5

Sports: Games People Played

One cultural element that marked the 1920s as the start of modern America was the full range of big-time spectator sports during the decade. An American society anything less than sports crazy cannot be considered "modern." Among the new heroes of the Jazz Age were tennis and golf stars of both sexes, women channel swimmers, and thoroughbred racehorses. Meanwhile, traditional sports heroes, such as baseball and football players, gained increasing fame and influence. Babe Ruth, Ty Cobb, and Red Grange became not just stars of the diamond and gridiron, but role models for the youth of a generation. In the early nineteenth century, American youth ordinarily found their heroes in politics—an Andrew Jackson, an Abraham Lincoln, or a Jefferson Davis. After the Civil War, heroes were more likely business tycoons such as Andrew Carnegie or John Rockefeller. After 1900 and the increasing popularity of spectator sports, however, athletic stars steadily replaced other types of heroes. Home Run Baker often replaced banker J. Pierpont Morgan in the adoring eyes of the young. By the late 1920s, a wide-ranging sports revolution had taken place.[1]

Breckenridge was right in swing with the national mania. Citizens not only rooted for national big city teams, they also turned out for countless local live exhibitions and games—from amateur boxing to cross-country racing. Moreover, they demonstrated the manic attachment to local high-school teams that Texas towns have always been famous for. In place of the Mojo Magic mystique of contemporary Odessa, Texas, Breckenridge fastened on its high-school "Buckaroos" and their female athletic counterparts—the "Buckarettes."[2]

Despite the intense local team loyalties, Breckenridge citizens increasingly followed more national sports. Radio broadcasting in the mid-1920s replaced the secondhand reports of newspapers and occasional semilive telegraph reporting of baseball scores to live audiences with truly live play-by-plays. Today, few Americans feel guilty about the predominance of sport. In the 1920s, spectator sports had far more critics, but they were quickly overwhelmed.

Heywood Hale Broun, the perceptive cultural critic, caught the changing tide aptly in his 1920 essay in *The Nation*. Broun dreamed that John Roach Stratton, a famous brimstone and hellfire preacher, had gone to heaven. Stratton asked God to rain fire on Yankee Stadium because the Yankees had attracted a crowd of forty thousand on a Sunday. But Broun suggested that, as Babe Ruth came up to bat, God told Stratton: "Let's at least wait until the inning is over."[3] America's and Breckenridge's big league baseball compulsion is, perhaps, the part of the 1920s sports craze most familiar to us today.

There is no evidence that Basil Clemons had a vital interest in sports, although he might well have been a bemused spectator. Clemons and his camera caught the hysteria without, evidently, his catching the fever.

Frank Starr Heavy Wt. Of Breckenridge, Presented By R. E. Biddy Mgr. Athletic Club.

Breckenridge heavyweight Frank Starr in publicity photo, 1922. It was not Jack Dempsey vs. Gene Tunney, but Breckenridge offered local fight fans a full twenty-eight-round boxing card with a twelve-round feature match.

Even tykes drew a boxing crowd in Breckenridge. The young fighter on the right, however, does not seem eager to start the match. These two, Chick Wilson and John Terry, Jr., were billed as the "lightest heavyweights in the world," 1922.

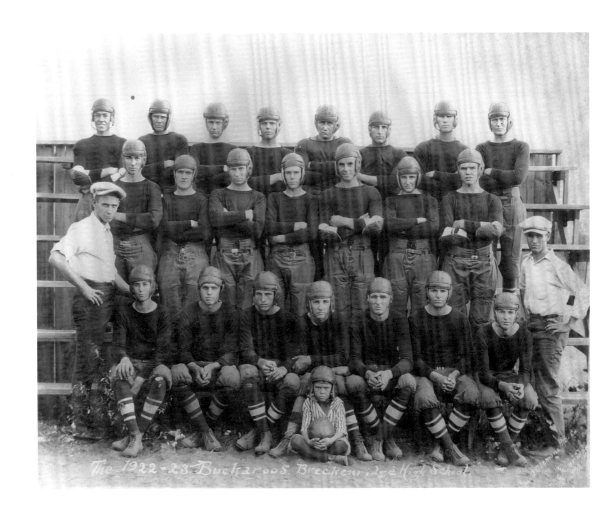

The Breckenridge High School football players wear appropriately ferocious expressions. Even the young mascot looks macho, 1922.

The Breckenridge High School girls' basketball team stresses their femininity with demure looks and girlish poses to offset the oft-perceived masculine image of women athletes. The 1920s made women channel swimmers and tennis players acceptably feminine but not women basketball players, 1929.

Bob Stilwell In His New Supecharged Mc Cathren Special Appearing In Oil Belt Fair Races. Sep. 28-30. Breckenridge, Tex.

Race car driver Bob Stilwell and his car, 1926.

African-American marathon runner, Tiger Flowers, 1929.

African-American baseball team from Breckenridge Baptist Church
assemble in full uniform, 1927. The 1930 federal census listed
426 African Americans in Breckenridge.

Baseball fans following 1921 World Series on electric scoreboard.

Getting Returns of Ft. Worth–Mobile
BaseBall Game. Sep. 1922 At The Shrine Club
Breckenridge, Tex.

Even minor-league games garnered an audience. Fans at Shrine Club
await scores from Fort Worth–Mobile baseball game, 1922.

CHAPTER 6

Frontier Flappers: Women and Fashion in the Oil Belt

If big-time spectator athletics were one important element of the national culture of the 1920s, the sexual revolution and women's emancipation were two other essential parts. Nationally, the women's movement never lived up to its political promise. Following World War I, the suffrage movement culminated in the Twenty-second Amendment, which gave women the right to vote. Although feminist leaders had promised that giving women the ballot would make America better, there was little immediate evidence of improvement. Instead, America got Warren Harding, Calvin Coolidge, and Herbert Hoover, while the Jazz Age brought better organized crime, bootleg liquor, and a move away from conventional social mores. It turned out that few women ran for office, and there was no measurable impact of women voting. Women tended to vote as their male relatives did or vice versa. Rich women voted unlike poor women, and Texas women voted differently than Iowa women.[1]

Women in Breckenridge did differ from national norms in one important way. As frontier women they had a heritage of independence, which was not as pronounced among their Eastern sisters. The frontier had always rewarded aggressiveness in women, and the West still tended to admire female tenacity far more than the East. Yet, increasingly, the mass media and mass culture blurred the cultural lines between East and West. Breckenridge women picked up fashions from the new national women's magazines and learned how to act from Hollywood actresses. Young women all over America had new heroines in the 1920s, embodied in female athletes and glamorous movie stars. These new heroines replaced older role models such as society women, social workers, and suffragettes.

Young women often found older women impossibly prudish about sex. The young flappers sought excitement not in struggling against social evils, but in breaking cultural taboos. Increasingly young women revolted against social conventions, often insisting on the right to smoke, drink, and choose their own sexual partners. Young women were liberated culturally by new national norms, yet most women were still trapped by economic reality. As they got older, the only alternatives for most were traditional marriages and home life. Youth was a passing condition: It offered women a new-found cultural freedom but not economic security.[2]

Breckenridge women illustrated national trends as they followed national fashions. There was still a Texas flavor to their lifestyles, but clearly mass culture was affecting them far more than they influenced the broader forces. In the 1920s, the small city became the cultural suburb of the large city, and Texas became the cultural apprentice of New York. With its sudden affluence, Breckenridge offered a clinic on the dynamics of cultural change. And in the 1920s, no other group was affected more than women. The generation gap, the revolution in clothing styles, and the sexual revolution all influenced the cultural self-portrait of women. In the nineteenth century, Easterners had tried to appear Western. In the 1920s, Westerners often tried to act Eastern. Clearly affluent Breckenridge women started to take more direct cues from the outside world, and Clemons's camera caught the subtle—and not so subtle—changes in women's dress, expression, roles, and attitudes.

Breckenridge female high school teachers in staid, schoolmarm dress
at the dawn of the Jazz Age, 1920.

Mother's Day group of Presbyterian women, seemingly not impressed by the revolution in manners and morals embodied by the flappers of the twenties, 1926.

Presbyterian women in a scene from their comedic production
with a suffrage theme, 1923.

Newsstand near the post office featuring mass circulation national magazines, 1927.

Young woman with beauty magazine, 1925. These magazines now preached that beauty was available to all but the lazy.

Lady barbers standing in front of their shop, 1920.

Beauty pageant winner Lillie Pearl Corley (Miss Breckenridge) poses at nearby Possum Kingdom Lake, 1929. Female beauty was equated with slimness by Ziegfeld showgirls around 1915 and reinforced by boyish fashions in the 1920s.

Young apprentice flappers make up the "Babyface Chorus" in a show
sponsored by the Breckenridge Elks, 1926.

Miss Mary Francis Russell 1927 Buckaroo Queen.

The 1927 Breckenridge High School prom queen,
Mary Francis Russell, sits on her throne.

CHAPTER 7

Main Street Breckenridge: Babbitts in Boomtown

In 1924, when President Calvin Coolidge proclaimed that "the business of America is business," most Breckenridge citizens would probably have said "amen." The city had already been fueled by four hectic years of nonstop business expansion. The nation's economic bullishness was punctuated by a steadily rising stock market that supposedly reflected America's bright economic future. By 1928, however, critics warned that the vastly inflated stock prices did not really forecast the future. Instead they only illustrated the instant gratification and profit of the moment. America was on the upside of a classic boom and bust.[1]

However, the Breckenridge boom was more solidly based. One did not have to be an economic forecaster to see that the growing population of workers and oil barons would need accommodations and services. The Breckenridge business community needed only to service the present; the future could take care of itself. From the largest oil magnate to the smallest shopkeeper, Breckenridge entrepreneurs believed that nothing could break the upward business spiral. Soon Breckenridge's Main Street was dotted with general stores, department stores, and restaurants, though among these stood less solidly financed enterprises such as speakeasies, fast-food stands and single-server cafes as well.

Breckenridge was a classic booster town. It incorporated both the traditional booster spirit of newly founded nineteenth-century Western towns and the optimistic, utopian capitalism of the 1920s. Older Western towns were usually led by a mayor and city council, composed of town merchants and entrepreneurs. The mayor might own the general store, while a council member might be the town blacksmith and another the town doctor or dentist. All these citizens were natural town boosters, for whatever was good for their town was good for business. Booster towns merged public and private interests, a fact evident in the word "businessman," which meant a public servant in nineteenth-century England. An Englishman who owned a private business was called a merchant. In Western booster towns, there was no clear line between private and public business. America invented our modern definition of the "businessman."[2]

American town boosters had one consuming goal—to draw as many new residents to their town as possible. Each new citizen would directly benefit boosters' stores or practices, while driving up the value of any real-estate holdings. Local newspapers were used primarily to bolster the town's image, seldom covering anything but local events and leaving national and state news to big urban dailies. It was not that these newspapers loved the world less, they just loved their town more. Since each town had its own booster press, America had more newspapers than any other nation. Also, most towns built a fancy hotel, specifically to impress visitors who were looking the area over.

Breckenridge had lost its nineteenth-century competition to other West Texas cities, such as Fort Worth, Abilene, and Lubbock, but oil gave Breckenridge another chance in the 1920s. The new, consuming capitalistic faith in American business enterprise helped fuel Breckenridge's modern booster spirit. The old style boosterism was now institutionalized in a local chamber of commerce. Yet, the town newspaper, the *Breckenridge American,* characteristically focused on the town's business growth. Also, by 1927, the new multistory Burch hotel towered above the town as a symbol of growth, a modern oasis for town visitors.

The 1924–25 Breckenridge city directory showed that the "babbitry" that Sinclair Lewis's novel, *Babbitt,*[3] had made a synonym for the new booster spirit was alive and well in Breckenridge. The directory displayed 110 advertisers, most of which were small businesses. They included ten auto dealers, nine lawyers, and the King Hospital (with "35 rooms and elevator service"). Private enterprise also provided Breckenridge with two domino parlors and thirty-one restaurants and cafes in 1924.[4]

Ironically, Basil Clemons did not advertise in the directory. Yet, an important part of Clemons's business was photographing business interiors and exteriors for ads and flyers. Probably entrepreneurs quickly heard of Clemons's excellent work and low prices by word of mouth. His work was also constantly displayed by the *Breckenridge American,* which often used Clemons as a freelance news photographer and printed his commercial photographs in stories and ads. Clemons lived among the "Main Street" crowd, surrounded by George Babbitt booster philosophy. Yet, even more clearly, Clemons never surrendered to it, though his photos promoted Main Street's boosterism. Clemons remained a boomtown Bohemian.

The Piggly Wiggly grocery chain originated in the Southeast and pioneered
self-service stores with mazelike aisles, 1923.

The Acorn clothing store's grand opening, 1927.

The JC Penney's department store, 1930.

The local Buick dealer, 1920.

Shorty's Lunch Room, short on almost everything but entrepreneurial faith, 1920.

The drive-in, 1920s style, 1926.

"The Bud" was short for "The Budweiser," a popular speakeasy
during the first year of Prohibition, 1921.

Charles Lugo (center) poses in his "Mexican Town" restaurant,
surrounded by customers. "Mexican Town" had its own Main Street
in Breckenridge and its own neighborhood, 1921.

Rush hour traffic jam in downtown Breckenridge, 1922.

Children working at the Farmer's Poultry & Egg Co. dressing plant, 1927.
Child labor laws passed in the early 1900s were poorly enforced all over America.

Ice stored at Alexander's Ice Plant for Breckenridge's "ice boxes," 1927.

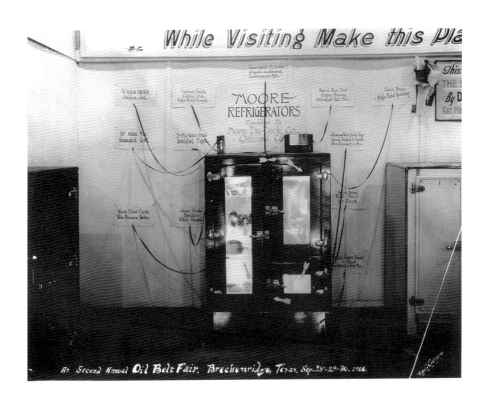

The Oil Belt Fair shows a deluxe new electric refrigerator
to replace the icebox, 1926.

Elks State Convention at the Burch hotel, 1929. The Burch was built in 1927
as Breckenridge's commercial centerpiece.

The Breckenridge Elks' float in the 1929 State Convention parade.

The Ku Klux Klan parades in Breckenridge, 1922. The Klan represented
the seamiest part of middle-class joiners in the twenties, and Klan membership per
capita in the 1920s was higher in the Southwest than in the South.

The Armistice Day Parade symbolized community solidarity and patriotism,
as opposed to the Klan, which encouraged division, terror, and intimidation, 1927.

Breckenridge Police Department, 1927.

"New American LaFrance Fire Engine," 1927.

The Van Zant Still. Captured By The Sherif's Department East of Breckenridge, Texas.

Sheriffs show off still, captured East of Breckenridge, 1927. Moonshiners were also entrepreneurs, especially during Prohibition.

CHAPTER 8

Faces Outside the Crowd: The People of Breckenridge

Rich and poor, black and white, Anglo and Hispanic, young and old, native and drifter, merchant and rancher, oil speculator and oilfield roughneck—they all looked out at Clemons's camera in search of a permanent souvenir for themselves or friends. Now these sixty-five- to seventy-five-year-old photographs look out at us. There are family groups and solitary portraits, but the key differentiations come from clothes and expression. Clothing furnishes clues to economic class, while expression tells us more about attitudes toward life, albeit in subtle coded ways that are open to interpretation. The clues are somewhat predictable, of course. Prosperous people usually dressed in expensive stylish accoutrements and wore smiles of satisfaction. Less affluent subjects often wore less-impressive clothes, but still often sported smiles of happiness. Stern looks suggested spartan or serious approaches to life; weathered faces suggested outdoor labor.

Clemons's portraits included a number of Mexican-American and African-American subjects and so did his group photos. Since the official minority population of Breckenridge was relatively small, the number of Clemons's minority photos is noteworthy. Clemons had a general reputation for making friends in all social, ethnic, and economic groups. Also his own spare, bottom-bunk lifestyle probably made him particularly sympathetic to minority groups, whose lifestyles were often similar. Clemons's photos of African Americans and Mexican Americans show no hint of condescension. Like his circus photographs, his minority photographs display a subtle affection and kinship. One can easily speculate that Clemons saw both circus people and minorities as cultural outsiders, much like himself.

The federal censuses of 1920 and 1930 missed Breckenridge's boom years. The 1920 census did not break down the Breckenridge population by race, although it did so for Stephens County, which included Breckenridge. The 1930 census listed Breckenridge's diminished official population as 7,569, which included 426 African Americans (5.6% of the population). It also listed 102 people in an "other races" category, which contained mostly Mexican-American citizens. The 1920 census did not list any races other than "Negro" and "White," and the latter included Mexican Americans. The actual Breckenridge minority population was likely understated, because minority workers (especially Mexican Americans and Mexican nationals) were more often seasonal workers or transients without a permanent address.[1]

Regardless of race or class, Clemons seldom posed his subjects in fanciful surroundings or artful groupings. Although there are some formal portraits, he usually shot them naturally, as they were. These informal portraits bear some resemblance to Richard Avedon's casual portraits in his book, *In the American West*.[2] Clemons's faces of West Texas run the social gamut and bring back the reality and feel of rural and small-town Texans in the Jazz Age. Yet, these personal photos also suggest how much we share with these people. Though mute and sometimes strangely clothed, these faces express the range of universal human emotions, dramatically portraying joy, suffering, pride, and resignation.

People usually look at the past as if looking through a window and into someone else's house—the surroundings are strange, but their arrangement feels somewhat familiar. However, suddenly and unpredictably, the past can just as easily become a mirror, and so it is with Clemons's portraits. We may recognize the expression, if not the face. We may sense the anguish, if not the specific cause. We may see the pride, if not the social basis. Portraits are especially haunting, because they seldom tell a full story—they spark our imaginations with the "what," but almost never satisfy our curiosity about the "why."

This is especially true of Clemons's photographs. Since he evidently did not write about his work and seldom talked about it, we may never know much more than what these photographs reveal. Looking at Clemons's photos tells us much about the 1920s and gives some insight into Clemons. Most of the physical subjects of Clemons's photos are external to the man himself. Yet, the way he photographed them—the subjects themselves, their expressions, their surroundings, and above all, what they evoke in us nearly eighty years later—suggest aspects of Clemons. These photos subtly tell us about the kind of man he was, and his perceptions of his times, as they bring back the times themselves.

Quartet of sheriffs at the Texas sheriffs' convention, 1921.

Fort Worth sheriff R. L. Van Story, winner of the "best marksman" shooting
contest at the sheriffs' convention in Breckenridge, 1927.

Mr. and Mrs. W. E. Reeding celebrating their "sixtieth honeymoon anniversary"
with a flight to Abilene on Braniff Airlines. Mr. Reeding (right)
was eighty-eight and his wife was eighty, 1927.

Rancher W. C. Blackmond with his prizewinning poultry, 1924.

W.C. Blachmond Of the Petaluma Ranch With One Of
His Prize Winners At Second Annual Poultry Show
Breckenridge, Texas. Oct. 7.8.9. 1924.

Basil Clemons Photo Co.

Within the image (handwritten): F.E. Simpson & Party With The Big Ones That Didn't Get Away Clearfork River, Breckenridge, Tex. 12 Pounds 20 Pounds

Three fishermen with their Clear Fork River catch, 1924.

Mexican-American family, 1925.

African-American Breckenridge patrons at the Dallas Cabaret, 1920.
These African-American juke joints were models for the 1930s Texas honky-tonks.

Jim, an employee at the Budweiser bar, and his dog King, 1921.

Coffin photo of three-year-old J. P. McGee, 1925.

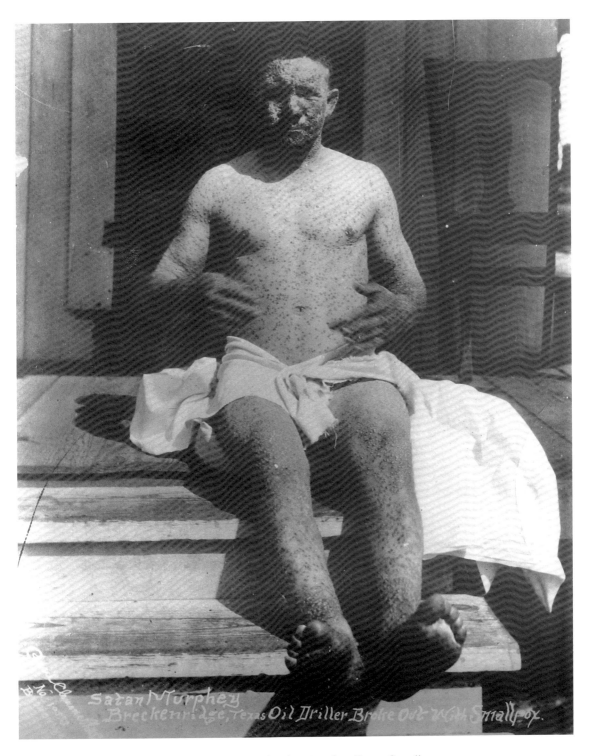

Oilfield worker, Satan Murphy, showing the effects of smallpox, 1921.

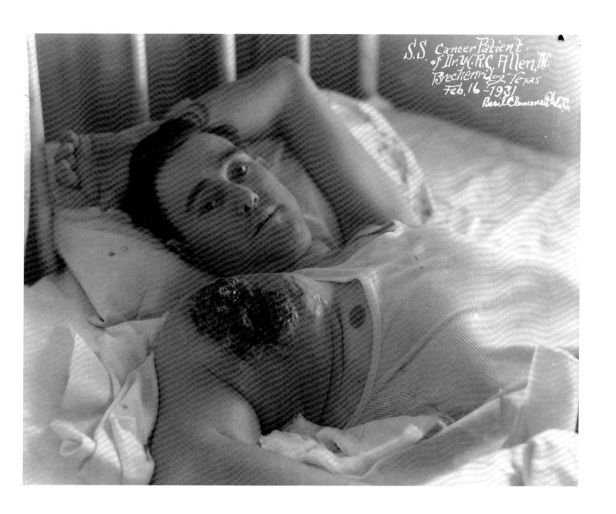

Patient with advanced cancerous tumor, 1931.

Dr. Swiney, a Breckenridge family doctor, beside the
Nash Special Coupe he used for house calls, 1926.

The annual Davis Family Reunion and Encampment
on the Clear Fork River, 1927.

Working-class family, ca. 1928.

The construction crew that built the Breckenridge High School. African-American
and Caucasian workers were united on the job, but clearly divided in this photo, 1922.

The Morris Bender family poses outside their home. Bender was a prosperous merchant who owned a Breckenridge department store bearing his name, ca. 1926.

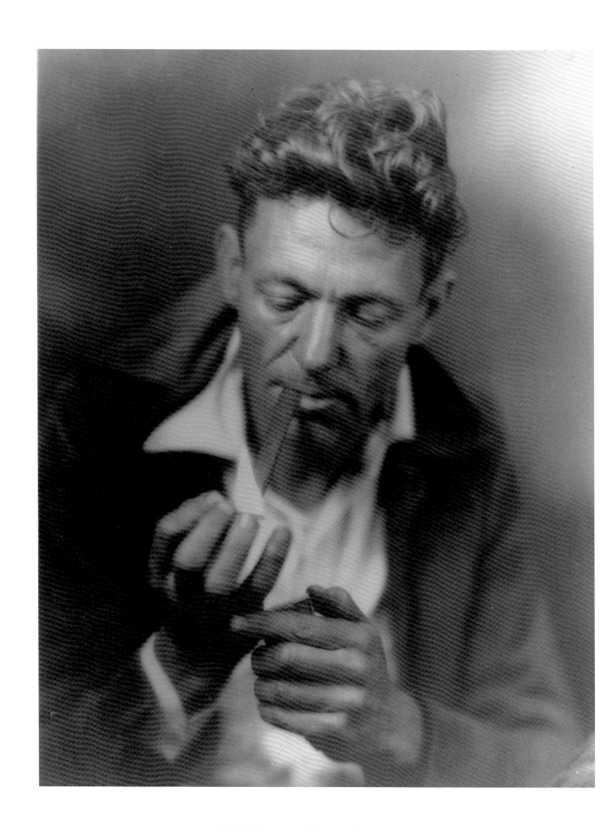

Basil Clemons, self-portrait, ca. 1920.

NOTES

CHAPTER 1
BASIL CLEMONS:
THE PHOTOGRAPHER AND THE MAN

1. Interviews with Max Goldblatt, May 23, 1988, in Arlington, Texas, and with Frank Pellizzari, Jr., in Breckenridge, June 12, 1988. Goldblatt knew Clemons when Goldblatt was a high-school student during the 1920s. Goldblatt moved to Dallas in the 1930s, became a successful businessman, and eventually served on the Dallas city council in the 1970s. Frank Pellizzari, Jr., helped Clemons with his photography business in the late 1920s and 1930s. Clemons's tent-wagon home was stationed on a vacant lot across the street from the Pellizzari home. Frank's family sometimes helped Clemons with food, water, and laundry in his early years in Breckenridge and on a regular basis when Clemons went blind in the 1950s.

2. Jean Ann (Pellizzari) Credicott, "Basil Edwin Clemons," unpublished copy of biographic note in The University of Texas at Arlington Libraries, Special Collections Division, Manuscript Holding File on the Basil Clemons Photograph Collection. Also, Jean Ann (Pellizzari) Credicott, biographical sketch of Basil Edwin Clemons in *The New Handbook of Texas,* 157.

3. Betty Elliott Hanna, *Doodle Bugs and Cactus Berries: A Historical Sketch of Stephens County,* 114–17.

4. Frank Pellizzari, Jr., interview, June 12, 1988.

CHAPTER 2
WEST TEXAS CRUDE:
BRECKENRIDGE AS AN OIL BOOMTOWN

1. Roger and Diana Olien, *Easy Money: Oil Promoters and Investors in the Jazz Age,* 37–38.

2. Loy William Hartsfield, "A Brief History of Breckenridge and the Stephens County Oil Fields," *West Texas Historical Association Yearbook,* 12 (July, 1936): 111–16. Also see *A Brief History of Stephens County* (Breckenridge, 1976).

3. Quoted in Hartsfield, "A Brief History of Breckenridge and the Stephens County Oil Fields," 111–12.

4. Ibid.

5. Max Goldblatt, interview, May 23, 1988. Also see Loy William Hartsfield, "A History

of Stephens County, Texas" (M.A. thesis, The University of Texas at Austin, 1929), 96–105.

CHAPTER 3
BREAD AND CIRCUSES:
ENTERTAINMENT OFF AND ON THE ROAD

1. Robert Bogdan, *Freak Show: Presenting Human Oddities for Amusement and Profit,* 69–77.
2. Jerome L. Rodnitzky, "Recapturing the West: The Dude Ranch in American Life," *Arizona and the West* 10 (Summer, 1968): 123–26.
3. Earl Pomeroy, *In Search of the Golden West,* 219–20.
4. Marshall McLuhan, *Understanding Media: The Extensions of Man,* vii–xi.

CHAPTER 4
THE FIRST PICTURE SHOW:
THE IMPACT OF CINEMA

1. Larry McMurtry, *The Last Picture Show.*
2. Larry May, *Screening Out the Past: The Birth of Mass Culture and the Motion Picture Industry.*
3. Arthur Knight, *The Liveliest Art: A Panoramic History of the Movies,* 107–42.
4. Marianne Triponi, "The New Ironwood Theatre in Context: Movie Palace As Symbol," *Journal of American Culture* 13 (Winter, 1990): 1–7.

CHAPTER 5
SPORTS:
GAMES PEOPLE PLAYED

1. Dixon Wecter, *The Hero in America;* Douglas Wallop, *Baseball: An Informal History.*
2. H. G. Bissinger, *Friday Night Lights.* This is a study of the modern and traditional fanatic approach to West Texas high-school football.
3. Heywood Hale Broun's essay quoted in Paul A. Carter, *The Twenties in America,* 22.

CHAPTER 6
FRONTIER FLAPPERS:
WOMEN AND FASHION IN THE OIL BELT

1. June Sochen, *Movers and Shakers: American Women Thinkers and Activists, 1900–1910.*
2. William O'Neill, *Everyone Was Brave;* William H. Chafe, *The American Woman: Her Changing Social, Economic, and Political Role, 1920–1970;* Lois Banner, *Women in Modern America,* 131–70.

CHAPTER 7
MAIN STREET BRECKENRIDGE:
BABBITS IN BOOMTOWN

1. For a good contemporary view of the 1920s business climate, see Frederick Lewis Allen, *Only Yesterday: An Informal History of the 1920s,* 102–88.
2. On nineteenth-century Western boosters, see Daniel Boorstin, *The Americans: The National Experience,* 113–68.
3. Sinclair Lewis, Sinclair Lewis, *Babbitt.*
4. *Hudspeth's Breckenridge Texas Directory, 1924–25.*

CHAPTER 8
FACES OUTSIDE THE CROWD:
THE PEOPLE OF BRECKENRIDGE

1. *Fifteenth Census of the United States, 1930, Population,* vol. 3, pt. 2, 939–1081.
2. Richard Avedon, *In the American West, 1979–1984.*

BIBLIOGRAPHY

Basil Clemons left researchers very little besides his photographs. There were apparently few personal papers or business records, and he had no wife, children, or business associates. What we know about him comes largely from the reminiscences of Breckenridge residents. The memories are warm and consistent, but seldom get very deep into Clemons's psyche. Clemons is remembered as friendly, independent, disinterested in material wealth, and above all wrapped up in photography. Offbeat is the image that most recollections of Clemons foster. The most specific information on Clemons comes from the Pellizzari family, who lived across the street from Clemons for many years. Particularly valuable are the memories of Frank Pellizzari, Jr., and the biographical sketches of Clemons by Pellizzari's daughter, Jean Ann (Pellizzari) Credicott.

If Clemons remains mysterious, boomtown Breckenridge does not. The city's history was captured not only in Clemons's photos, but by a vigorous newspaper, the *Breckenridge American,* and some competent historical writing. Loy William Hartsfield's 1929 master's thesis, "A History of Stephens County, Texas" is the essential starting place for tracing Breckenridge's past. His 1936 article, "A Brief History of Breckenridge and the Stephens County Oil Fields," zeroes in on the 1920s. The town newspaper, of course, provides the most specific details on Breckenridge history and is available on microfilm at the Breckenridge Public Library.

There are many useful books that cover the Texas oil booms and Texas social life in the 1920s. Among the best are Roger and Diana Olien, *Easy Money: Oil Promoters and Investors in the Jazz Age,* Joe Frantz, *Texas: A Bicentennial History,* Richard R. Moore, *West Texas after the Discovery of Oil,* and Mody C. Boatright and William A. Owens, *Tales from the Derrick Floor: A People's History of the Oil Industry. Life in the Oil Fields,* by Roger and

Diana Olien, is based on dozens of interviews with former oilfield workers and is particularly good at capturing the flavor of boomtowns. The Oliens' *Oil Booms: Social Change in Five Texas Towns* does not furnish specific information on Breckenridge but does attack and largely destroy the exaggerated, violent image of oil boomtowns, created by Hollywood films and sensational journalism. Norman D. Brown's *Hood, Bonnet and Little Brown Jug: Texas Politics, 1921–1928* is particularly good on Texas town cultural life in the 1920s (from the Ku Klux Klan to Prohibition) that had political ramifications.

National culture during the twenties has been richly addressed by scholars and novelists alike. Jazz-Age culture was such a striking departure that cultural critics wrote about it profusely from the start. Indeed, the most vivid depictions of the Jazz Age often come from those contemporary observers. Among the best of this genre are novels such as F. Scott Fitzgerald's *The Great Gatsby* and *This Side of Paradise* and Sinclair Lewis's, *Main Street* and *Babbitt*. Also noteworthy are journalist Frederick Lewis Allen's *Only Yesterday: An Informal History of the 1920s* and a collection of contemporary articles in George Mowry's *The Twenties: Fords, Flappers, and Fanatics*. Among the most useful works of recent cultural scholarship on the 1920s are Paul A. Carter's *Another Part of the Twenties* and Frederick J. Hoffman's *The 20's*.

SOURCES

UNPUBLISHED

Credicott, Jean Ann (Pellizzari). "Basil Edwin Clemons," unpublished biographic note. Basil Clemons Photograph Collection (ms. holding file), The University of Texas at Arlington Libraries, Special Collections Division.

Goldblatt, Max. Interview with Jerry L. Rodnitzky. Arlington, Texas, May 23, 1988.

Hartsfield, Loy William. "A History of Stephens County, Texas." Master's thesis, University of Texas at Austin, 1929.

Pellizzari, Frank, Jr. Interview with the authors. Breckenridge, Texas, June 12, 1988.

Rodnitzky, Shirley R. "A Guide to the Basil Clemons Photograph Collection." The University of Texas at Arlington Libraries, Special Collections Division, Arlington, Texas.

PUBLISHED

Abbott, Carl. *Urban America in the Modern Age: 1920 to the Present.* Arlington Heights, Ill.: Harlan Davidson, 1987.

Adams, Ansel. *Ansel Adams: Letters and Images, 1916–1984.* Boston: Little, Brown, 1988.

Allen, Frederick Lewis. *Only Yesterday: An Informal History of the 1920s.* New York: Harper and Row, 1931.

Avedon, Richard. *In the American West, 1979–1984.* New York: Abrams, 1985.

Banner, Lois. *Women in Modern America.* New York: Harcourt, Brace, Jovanovich, 1974.

Bissinger, H. G. *Friday Night Lights.* New York: Addison-Wesley, 1990.

Boatright, Mody and Owens, William A. *Tales From the Derrick Floor: A Peoples History of the Oil Industry.* Garden City, N.Y.: Doubleday, 1970.

Bogdan, Robert. *Freak Show: Presenting Human Oddities for Amusement and Profit.* Chicago: University of Chicago Press, 1988.

Boorstin, Daniel. *The Americans: The National Experience.* New York: Random House, 1967.

Breckenridge American, 1921–29. Breckenridge, Texas.

A Brief History of Stephens County. Breckenridge, Texas: Breckenridge Chamber of Commerce, 1976.

Brown, Norman D. *Hood, Bonnet, and Little Brown Jug: Texas Politics, 1921–1928.* College Station: Texas A&M University Press, 1984.

Carter, Paul A. *Another Part of the Twenties.* New York: Columbia University Press, 1977.

————. *The Twenties in America.* New York: Thomas V. Crowell Co., 1975.

Chafe, William H. *The American Woman: Her Changing Social and Political Role, 1920–1970.* New York: Oxford University Press, 1972.

Credicott, Jean Ann (Pellizzari), biographical sketch of Basil Edwin Clemons in *The New Handbook of Texas.* Austin: Texas State Historical Association, 1996.

Fifteenth Census of the United States, 1930, Population. Vol. 3, pt. 2. Washington: U.S. Government Printing Office, 1932.

Fitzgerald, F. Scott. *The Great Gatsby.* New York: Charles Scribner's Sons, 1925.

————. *This Side of Paradise.* New York: Charles Scribner's Sons, 1920.

Frantz, Joe. *Texas: A Bicentennial History.* New York: Norton, 1976.

Hanna, Betty Elliott. *Doodle Bugs and Cactus Berries: A Historical Sketch of Stephens County.* N.p.: Nortex Press, [1975].

Hartsfield, Loy William. "A Brief History of Breckenridge and the Stephens County Oil Fields." *West Texas Historical Association Yearbook* 12 (July, 1936): 100–23.

Hoffman, Frederick J. *The 20's.* New York: Macmillan, 1962.

House, Boyce. *Were You in Ranger?* Dallas: Tardy Publishing, 1935.

————. *Roaring Ranger.* San Antonio: Naylor Company, 1951.

Hudspeth's Breckenridge Texas Directory 1924–25. El Paso: Hudspeth Co., 1924.

Jeffrey, Walter H. *Deep Well Drilling.* Houston: Gulf Publishing Co., 1925.

Kasson, John F. *Amusing the Million.* New York: Farrow, Straus, and Giroux, 1978.

Knight, Arthur. *The Liveliest Art: A Panoramic History of the Movies.* New York: Macmillan Co., 1957.

Lesy, Michael. *Real Life: Louisville in the Twenties.* New York: Pantheon Books, 1976.

————. *Wisconsin Death Trip.* New York: Pantheon Books, 1973.

Lewis, Sinclair. *Babbitt.* New York: Harcourt, Brace and Co., 1922.

————. *Main Street.* New York: Harcourt, Brace and Co., 1920.

McLuhan, Marshall. *Understanding Media: The Extensions of Man.* New York: Signet, 1969.

McMurtry, Larry. *The Last Picture Show.* New York: Dial Press, 1966.

May, Larry. *Screening Out the Past: The Birth of Mass Culture and the Motion Picture Industry.* Chicago: University of Chicago Press, 1950.

Moore, Richard R. *West Texas After the Discovery of Oil.* Austin: Jenkins Publishing Co., 1971.

Mowry, George E., ed. *The Twenties: Fords, Flappers and Fanatics.* Englewood Cliffs, N.J.: Prentice Hall, 1963.

Olien, Roger M. and Diana D. *Easy Money: Oil Promoters and Investors in the Jazz Age.* Chapel Hill: University of North Carolina Press, 1990.

————. *Life in the Oil Fields.* Austin: Texas Monthly Press, 1986.

————. *Oil Booms: Social Change in Five Texas Towns.* Lincoln: University of Nebraska Press, 1982.

————. *Wildcatters: Texas Independent Oilmen.* Austin: Texas Monthly Press, 1984.

O'Neill, William. *Everyone Was Brave.* Chicago: Quadrangle Press, 1969.

Pomeroy, Earl. *In Search of the Golden West.* New York: Random House, 1952.

Richman, J. C. *Racing Bits.* Boston: R. G. Badger, 1926.

Rister, Carl Coke. *Oil: Titan of the Southwest.* Norman: University of Oklahoma Press, 1949.

Rodnitzky, Jerome L. "Recapturing the West: The Dude Ranch in American Life." *Arizona and the West* 10 (Summer, 1968): 123–26.

Rundell, Walter. *Early Texas Oil.* College Station: Texas A&M University Press, 1977.

————. "Photographs As Historical Evidence." *American Archivist* 41 (October, 1978): 373–98.

Sochen, June. *Movers and Shakers: American Women Thinkers and Activists, 1900–1910.* New York: Quadrangle Books, 1973.

Soule, George. *Prosperity Decade: From War to Depression, 1918–1929.* New York: Rinehart, 1947.

Texas Almanac and State Industrial Guide. Dallas: A. H. Belo Corporation, 1919–1930.

Triponi, Marianne. "The New Ironwood Theatre in Context: Movie Palace As Symbol." *Journal of American Culture* 13 (Winter, 1990): 1–7.

Truzzi, Marcello. "Circuses, Carnivals, and Fairs in America." *Journal of Popular Culture* 6 (March, 1973): 529–34.

Vidich, Arthur J., and Joseph Bensman. *Small Town in Mass Society.* Princeton: Princeton University Press, 1968.

Wallop, Douglas. *Baseball: An Informal History.* New York: W. W. Norton, 1969.

Wecter, Dixon. *The Hero in America.* New York: Charles Scribner's Sons, 1941.

Whisenhunt, Donald W., ed. *Texas: A Sesquicentennial Celebration.* Austin: Eakin Press, 1984.

INDEX

Note: Pages with illustrations are indicated by italics.